Water Conflicts and Cooperation:
A media handbook

Funded by

Ministry of Foreign Affairs of the Netherlands

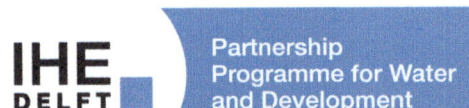

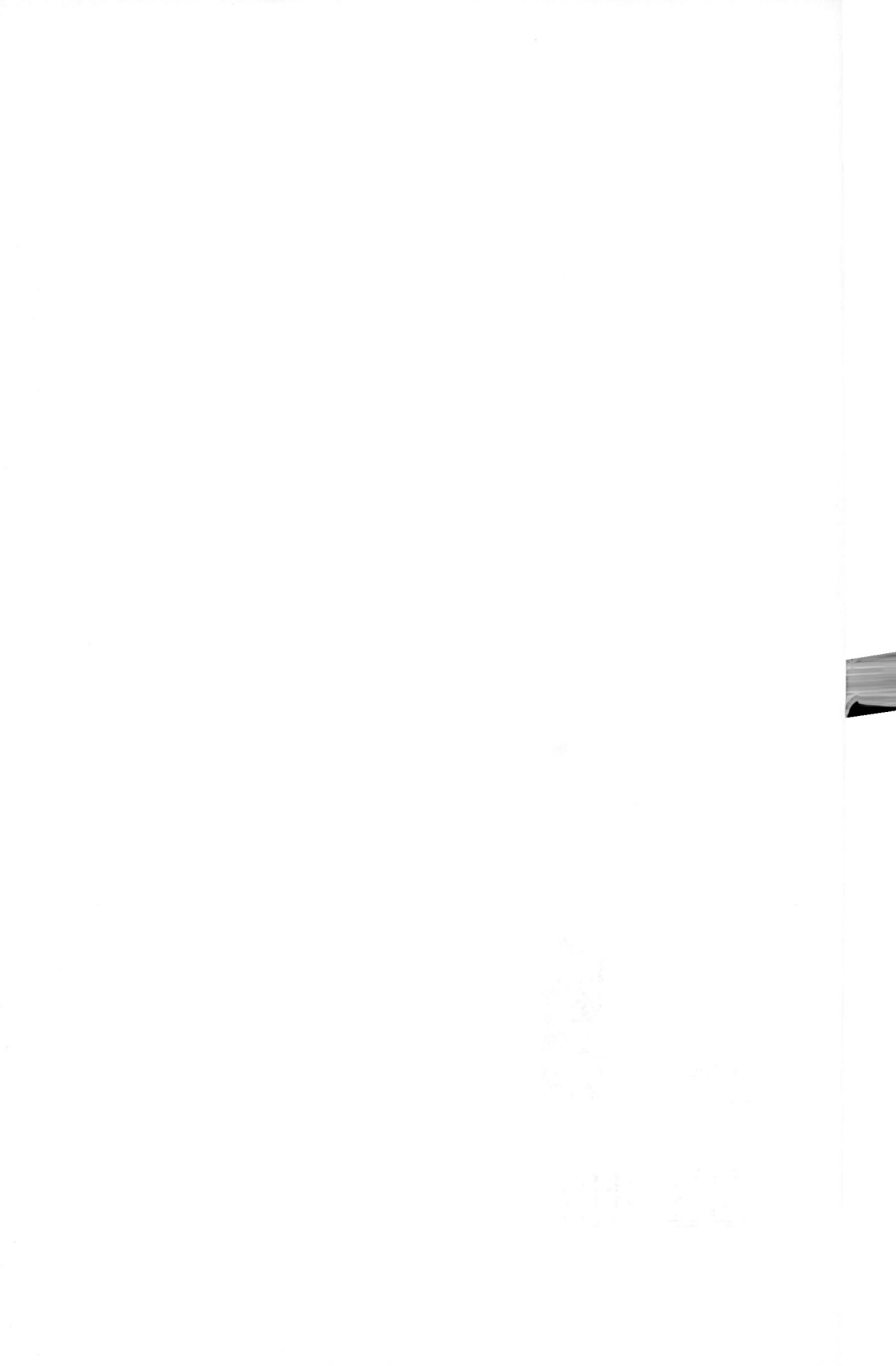

Water Conflicts and Cooperation:
A media handbook

Edited by Rasha Dewedar

CABI is a trading name of CAB International

CABI
Nosworthy Way
Wallingford
Oxfordshire OX10 8DE
UK

CABI
745 Atlantic Avenue
8th Floor
Boston, MA 02111
USA

Tel: +44 (0)1491 832111
Fax: +44 (0)1491 833508
E-mail: info@cabi.org
Website: www.cabi.org

Tel: +1 (617)682-9015
E-mail: cabi-nao@cabi.org

© CAB International 2021. All rights reserved. No part of this publication may be reproduced in any form or by any means, electronically, mechanically, by photocopying, recording or otherwise, without the prior permission of the copyright owners.

A catalogue record for this book is available from the British Library, London, UK.

Library of Congress Cataloging-in-Publication Data

Names: Dewedar, Rasha, editor.
Title: Water conflicts and cooperation : a media handbook / edited by Rasha Dewedar.
Description: Boston, MA : CAB International, [2021] | Includes bibliographical references and index. | Summary: "This handbook is for journalists, researchers and policy makers that are interested in working on science communication for water peace and cooperation, by detailing many activities implemented by the Open Water Diplomacy project in the Nile basin"-- Provided by publisher.
Identifiers: LCCN 2020031936 (print) | LCCN 2020031937 (ebook) | ISBN 9781789247954 (paperback) | ISBN 9781789247961 (ebook) | ISBN 9781789247978 (epub)
Subjects: LCSH: Mass media--Africa--Handbooks, manuals, etc. | Nile River Watershed--Press coverage. | Nile River Watershed--Water rights.
Classification: LCC DT115 .W335 2021 (print) | LCC DT115 (ebook) | DDC 333.9100962--dc23
LC record available at https://lccn.loc.gov/2020031936
LC ebook record available at https://lccn.loc.gov/2020031937

ISBN-13: 9781789247954 (paperback)
9781789247961 (ePDF)
9781789247978 (ePub)

DOI: 10.1079/9781789247954.0000

Commissioning editor: David Hemming
Editorial assistant: Ali Thompson
Production editor: James Bishop

Typeset by SPI, Pondicherry, India
Printed and bound in the UK by CPI Group (UK) Ltd, Croydon, CR0 8YY

Contents

1. **Introduction:** Water reporting, let your story flow   1
2. **Beyond Politics, Knowledge Bridge in Indus Basin**   3
3. **Reporting on Water Diplomacy:** Does Gender Matter?   9
4. **The Minister, the Prophet and God's Eye:** Scientists' voices in Nile media reporting   13
5. **Covering Water in Times of Conflict**   17
6. **Water Reporting:** Beyond dry pieces, nurture your coverage   23
7. **Reporting Shared Narratives:** Establishing transboundary cooperation through media   28
8. **Media and Water, is the Glass Half Full?**   34
9. **Satisfy People's Thirst for Information:** SIWI experience in training water journalists   38
10. **Science Communication Skills for Water Coverage:** Case study: IHE-SciDev Training   43

This handbook was coordinated by SciDev.Net, with support from the Programmatic Cooperation between the Directorate-General for International Cooperation (DGIS) of the Dutch Ministry of Foreign Affairs and IHE Delft in the period 2016–2020, also called DUPC2.

Author Biographies

Rasha Dewedar is a science writer and translator, with more than 14 years of experience in writing news and features on science, culture, lifestyle and gender issues, to different local and international portals. She worked with Nature Middle East, SciDev.Net, Scientific American, al-Arabiya.net, among others.

She holds a Master's degree in gender and development.

E-mail address: rashadewedar@hotmail.com

Alan Nicol: is the director of International Water Management Institute (IWMI) Strategic Program on Water, Growth and Inclusion. He is based at IWMI's East Africa Regional Office in Addis Ababa, Ethiopia. A political scientist by background, Alan has more than 25 years of experience of water research, policy advice, and program development in Asia, Africa and the Middle East. Email: A.Nicol@cgiar.org

Nitasha Nair: is a policy and management professional, with a unique experience in Branding, Communications, IT and Data Analytics. She holds a Master of Public Administration from Columbia University, where she studied energy and environment policy. She worked with the International Water Management Institute (CGIAR) from 2013-2017, and currently works as a Data Analytics consultant in the energy space. Email: nitasha.nair@gmail.com

Jenniver Sehring: is senior lecturer in Water Governance and Diplomacy at IHE Delft since 2018. Before that, she worked both in academia and with international actors on water-related aspects of security and water cooperation, particularly in Central Asia. Email: j.sehring@un-ihe.org

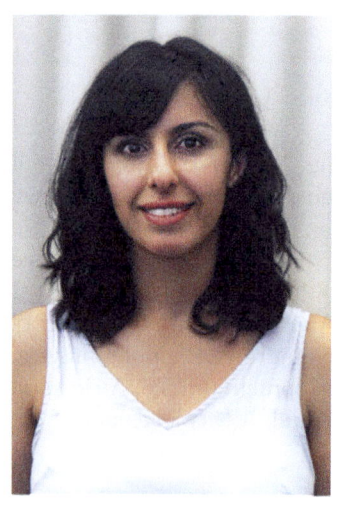

Alexandra Said: is programme officer for the Transboundary Water Cooperation Dept. and the International Centre for Water Cooperation (ICWC) at SIWI. Her focus areas include water governance in relation to gender and security, inclusive processes, and gender mainstreaming in the Nile basin. Email: alexandra.said@siwi.org

Author Biographies

Rozemarijn ter Horst: is a lecturer in water diplomacy at IHE Delft. Before her work with IHE Delft, Rozemarijn worked as freelance consultant on water governance, conflict and project management. Email: r.terhorst@un-ihe.org

Emanuele Fantini: is senior lecturer and researcher at the Department of Water Governance of IHE Delft Institute for Water Education (The Netherlands). He coordinates the project "Open Water Diplomacy. Media, science and transboundary cooperation in the Nile basin". Email: e.fantini@un-ihe.org

Ayah Aman: is a senior journalist at Al-Shorouk, Egyptian daily newspaper, and freelance writer, with 10 years' experience, graduated from the Faculty of Mass Communication, Cairo University. She travelled to most Nile Basin countries, covering historical, political, regional, and social aspects of the river and its people. Email: ayahaman88@gmail.com

Elzahraa Jadallah: is a writer and a freelance journalist based in Sudan. She worked previously as a TV producer/presenter and translator.

She has 6 years' experience in journalism in general and has been reporting on water and the environment since 2016. She is a former member of Sudanese Writers Union. Email: elzahraaibrahim@gmail.com

Frederick Mugira: Ugandan award-winning water and climate change journalist, has received the CNN/Multichoice African Journalist award and the UN Development Journalism Award. He is a media trainer and development communication specialist. He is currently the CEO for Water Journalists Africa and co-founder of InfoNile, a GeoJournalism platform that maps data on water issues in the Nile River basin. Email: mugifred@gmail.com

Rehab Abdalmohsen: is a bilingual freelance science journalist, writing news and features for several regional and international portals, like SciDev.Net, Scientific American, and the Niles; with a focus on covering water issues in the MENA region.

She has been awarded media best story from the World Health Organization on her coverage of anti-microbial resistance as a consequence of antibiotics overuse. Email: rehab.abdalmohsen@gmail.com

Kerry Schneider: has been working for the Stockholm International Water Institute (SIWI) since 2013, with the Transboundary Water Cooperation Department, where he manages the "Shared Waters Partnership", a multi-stakeholder platform aimed at advancing cooperation over shared water resources in regions where water is or could become a source of conflict. Email: Kerry.Schneider@siwi.org

Dr Charles Wendo: holds an MA in Journalism and Communication, a PGD in Mass Communication, and a Bachelor's degree in Veterinary Medicine. He is a science journalist, media trainer and Training Coordinator for SciDev.Net. He has worked for New Vision newspaper in Uganda and as a communication specialist for the Infectious Diseases Institute of Makerere University in Uganda. Email: charles.wendo@scidev.net

Introduction
Water reporting, let your story flow

By Rasha Dewedar
Freelance journalist

Water is that flood of generosity that gives life and prosperity; the fluid that runs through our bodies and interferes with our entire lives; that integral part of economy, politics, climate, environment and much more.

Reporting water is such a tough job that needs competent, knowledgeable and experienced journalists; it is just another form of science reporting that should be based on facts and data, rather than assumptions and opinions.

When information is all over the internet, and every day presents new challenges and increased competitiveness, journalists should focus on having an edge, an advantage over the others, new data, innovative coverage, human stories, etc.

Amid ever-changing contexts and continuously evolving tools, journalists should always be ready to embrace new changes, learn latest knowledge and use available tools to present science – and practise a lot!

This handbook is an endeavour to gather the expertise of people from different disciplines, genders, backgrounds and countries, who all work in the field of water diplomacy and water reporting. It aims at providing clearer understanding of the interaction between media, science and politics and its impact on water diplomacy, and how to cover water issues from a cooperative rather than a national interests point of view.

The target audience of the handbook is journalists, editors and researchers, as well as policy makers and media development organizations that are interested in working on science communication for water, peace and cooperation, and those who are searching for ideas and inspiration.

The configuration of the book and the selection of themes reflect the editorial board's vision of offering essential knowledge, perceived as substantial for water journalists' and communicators' work. It highlights academic insights, field work, case studies and best practices, presenting a wide range of opinions and expertise.

It also features descriptions and reflections of activities (action research, training modules, joint workshops, etc.), implemented in the Nile Basin, as well as success stories in other river basins.

The book is divided into three sections, each encompassing three chapters, as follows:

- Section One: Research on the role of media in water diplomacy.
- Section Two: Experiences of communication and reporting on water conflicts and cooperation.
- Section Three: Training media and journalists.

The first section or theme of the book gives a background on water diplomacy and how it intersects with gender inclusiveness, sheds light on the inspiring experience of 'Informing Change in the Indus Basin', and analyses how journalists represent scientists and use their quotes; it explores different representations of scientists in media coverage of Nile issues, reflecting on the different ideas on the role of science in the public debate that underpin such representations.

The second section focuses more on experiences of communication and reporting on water conflicts and cooperation; it offers insights on covering sensitive issues, going beyond national interest, and how journalists can address key issues, in a way that informs constructive policies and boosts transboundary cooperation.

The third section includes practical tips and tricks for water reporting, with a case study of an online course, aiming at building researchers' capacity to communicate science to journalists and other audiences, what they want to communicate, to whom and how to carve a communication strategy and plan.

This handbook has been developed within the project, 'Open Water Diplomacy. Media, science and transboundary cooperation in the Nile basin', funded by the Dutch Ministry of Foreign Affairs – Global Partnership for Water and Development and implemented by IHE Delft Institute for Water Education, SciDev.Net, Nile Basin Capacity Building Network, Africa Water Journalists and the University of Witwatersrand. The project aims at offering a space where water journalists and water scientists from different Nile Basin countries can get acquainted and engage in a process of common learning and co-production of knowledge and new narratives on the River Nile.

The experiences, projects and ideas here presented are not an exhaustive list. Rather the aim is to elicit conversation and collaboration between journalists, researchers and policy makers towards a constructive communication on water issues. A podcast series will integrate the handbook to keep the conversation flowing and stimulate new connections.

As actions speak louder than words, we hope that our words inspire both journalists and scientists to take a step towards the other, scientists making their findings simple and accessible for journalists and journalists being very careful with presenting scientific data and experts' quotes.

While appreciating water's bounties, let's never forget our role in preserving a continuous flow of correct information, offering generous data and maintaining a continuous stream of stories that nurture awareness and responsibility.

Beyond Politics, Knowledge Bridge in Indus Basin

2

By Alan Nicol[1] and Nitasha Nair[2]
[1]*Director of the International Water Management Institute (IWMI);*
[2]*Engagement Manager at Mu Sigma; MPA, Columbia University*

Fig. 2.1. Sayed Sharif Shobair from FAO explains hydrological cycle in the Kabul Basin at the Regional Media Dialogue in Kathmandu. Photo courtesy of International Water Management Institute (IWMI).

How can media play an active role in raising collective understanding of complex environmental topics in a politically charged basin?

This question is of utmost significance, and the beginning of any discussions or endeavors to train journalists on water issues. This is where the set of initiatives had started under 'Informing Change in the Indus Basin', a DFID funded project under the South Asia Water Governance Programme.

Throughout the project, the International Water Management Institute and its partners have been engaged with media across the Basin, to expose journalists to key research, and explore complex topics including water and climate change. This chapter presents a case study, analysing the context, challenges and lessons learnt from this experience.

Progressive Role

Shared by Afghanistan, China, India and Pakistan – four countries with histories of belligerence, three nuclear-armed, two at a state of war and one crippled by internal conflict – the Indus Basin is situated in a zone of acute geopolitical significance.

Growing populations, rapid urbanization and increasing competition for water between sectors are just some of the challenges facing the Indus Basin, which includes the world's largest contiguous irrigation scheme and has been a location of intensive agriculture for several millennia.

Within this context, the media shape and reinforce development narratives in multiple ways. Whilst often defaulting to reports of political mudslinging between countries (usually, but not exclusively, between India and Pakistan), the media can also play a more progressive role in raising awareness about issues, influencing public debates and policies and helping 'raise the game' in science journalism. This role as knowledge broker can help build bridges between countries, facilitating new flows of information and shifting narratives on crucial resource issues from vitriol to collaboration, and from a simplistic zero-sum analysis to more nuanced understandings about co-dependency across a shared geographical space.

Overview of Coverage and Challenges

The Indus Basin hosts a diverse range of media outlets across languages and mediums. There are varying degrees of restrictions on the media across the four countries, and these can fluctuate over time, depending on prevailing politics.

At the outset of the ICIB project, it was noted that coverage of Indus-related news remained largely event- rather than issue-based.

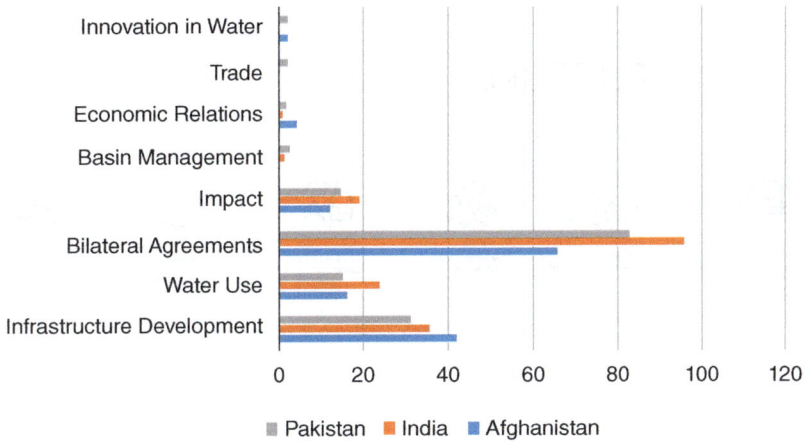

Fig. 2.2. Comparison of aspects covered on Indus. (Source: CARMA 2018.) Commissioned by IWMI under ICIB, a study by CARMA analysed 850 news stories in Pakistan between February 2016 and November 2016 1802 news articles in India between June 2016 and December 2016 and 50 news stories in Afghanistan between July 2016 and January 2017. Figure courtesy of International Water Management Institute (IWMI).

With media coverage in the region largely focused on overtly nationalistic and near-sighted issues of political conflict and inter-governmental dispute, ICIB identified an urgent need for journalists to understand connections between countries that went beyond conventional disputes, and included more developmental, shared and longer-term structural challenges affecting the whole basin population.

Mitigation Method

The Indus media work was a part of a larger programme, 'Informing Change in the Indus Basin' (ICIB). (See Fig. 2.3).

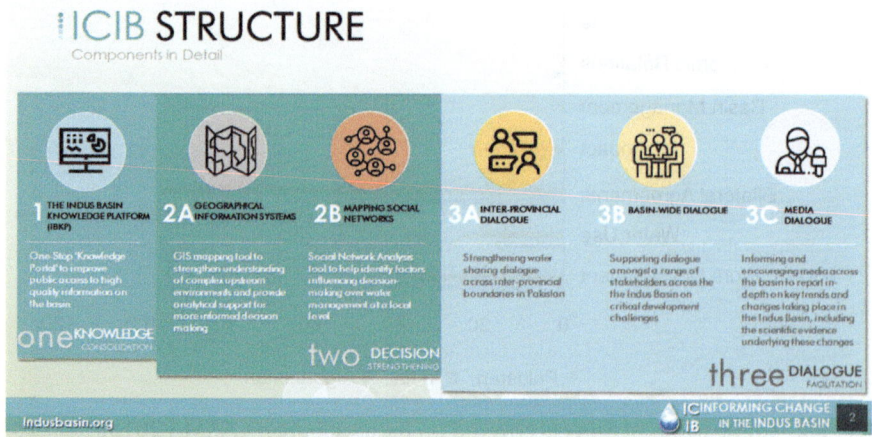

Fig. 2.3. Design elements of Indus Media Work. Figure courtesy of International Water Management Institute (IWMI).

Process and Structure of Interactions

The core of the Indus media component was a series of media dialogues which sought to expose journalists to different perspectives through interaction with the science and policy community. The content of the discussion included topics ranging from food security and research on climate to socio-economic change and the impact of policies on water demand. The key point was that experts simplified the science behind underlying trends and structural changes taking place in the Indus basin and could be further questioned by journalists.

The dialogues were first held at regional level. In order to reach out to more journalists, we expanded the model and organized four national-level media dialogues, including greater attention to the vernacular media (used by a larger segment of the population) and local experts.

These engagements were through multiple interactive sessions, typically over a couple of days, followed by a field trip to relevant local sites. The interactive sessions were held in a conference-style setup, including presentations, panel discussions and Q&A sessions with experts. We had also allocated time for group work where journalists were paired with experts, to come up with story ideas which were then pitched to an editor from the thirdpole.net (TTP). The editor would then offer instant feedback.

Right Partners and Participants

Partnership with like-minded organizations was key to the initiative's success. We collaborated with partners, including TTP, who not only brought a journalistic vision and perspective, but had also helped increase participation of the journalists in the initiative through their extensive networks. TTP was instrumental in the design and facilitation of the media dialogue sessions and media fellowships, and they have further provided a platform for the journalists to publish their stories.

We have also partnered with scientific institutions like ICIMOD (International Centre for Integrated Mountain Development), the Chinese Academy of Science and WWF (World Wild Fund for Nature), to highlight the latest research on the Indus and add scientific rigour to discussions. In addition, government and policy partners such as the Ministry of Energy and Water (MEW) in Afghanistan and the Water and Environment Forum in Pakistan added further credibility and legitimacy to the initiatives.

As for the media participants, we invited journalists who had covered environment or Indus-related issues in the past, reaching out to both senior editors as well as regular correspondents. By engaging senior editors, our aim was that knowledge would trickle down throughout the organization. The selected pool spread across print, broadcast and multimedia, with the mix being slightly different for each country.

Neutrality

Given the sensitive nature of the basin and its historical tensions, we designed the interactions to actively encourage a 'beyond politics' view. This was done by setting the purpose of the initiative to be issues of common interest affecting all, regardless of borders. We created safe spaces that encouraged the journalists to interact, where they could ask experts critical and often controversial questions. The experts in turn were encouraged to simplify their messages using as little jargon as possible in communicating key issues.

Some journalists funded themselves to overcome any potential conflict of interest, as some publications discourage journalists from being paid by an organization to attend a conference and then write about issues related to the funding organization. Further, the organizers ensured that participating in the Indus media dialogues was based on a 'no-strings-attached' policy and journalists were entirely free to pursue stories within the overall framework of the focus on development, climate change and the environment.

To foster further collaboration across borders, ICIB awarded 10 fellowships to journalists in all four Indus countries.

Sustainability Focus

ICIB integrated certain strategies to help sustain the momentum generated. This included leveraging social media platforms like WhatsApp, WeChat and Facebook to build on the dialogues, and prompt continued conversation between participants. Both national and regional groups were created to provide a neutral space to discuss issues of interest. In 2020 the social media groups were still being used to share articles and opinions, seek feedback from experts, and ask for contacts or even specific information.

Partnerships with like-minded organizations helped in creating a multiplier effect as some of the organizations such as the Ministry of Energy and Water (MEW) conducted further media events in Afghanistan, beyond the project, but using a similar format and including material shared during the ICIB media dialogues.

Impact and Opportunities

1. Leveraging social media: its impact and utility came into focus when Indus-related news hit the headlines in September 2016. Political decisions taken by the Indian government resulted in mud-slinging between India and Pakistan in which the Indus Waters Treaty became a focus area. Given the sensitive nature of the treaty, prior interaction between journalists and experts helped in facilitating debates and sharing different perspectives across the two countries. The WhatsApp group was used as a platform to discuss and understand the ramifications of these and other decisions beyond national borders. Experts felt more comfortable to engage and share research or opinions, which was critical for journalists who were operating to tight deadlines. As a result, and according to their own testimonies, journalists under the ICIB Media Component, both in India and Pakistan, were more measured in their reporting and published pieces which incorporated different perspectives.
2. Building community: we constituted a group of over 90 journalists over a period of three years from the four basin countries. Testimonies from journalists confirm that the interactions with media professionals in other countries helped in sharing tips and challenges of reporting Indus-related issues. Some of the journalists and experts have become good friends and are still in contact. However, given the wide expanse of media in the Indus countries, this number is only a beginning.
3. Coverage in high impact publications: the Indus media work resulted in a number of publications in well-read international, national and vernacular media outlets. The list includes *Nature, SciDev.Net* and the Hindi Water Portal to name a few. A story which was as a result of the ICIB fellowship was also a finalist in the 2018 American Geophysical Union's Walter Sullivan Award for Excellence in Science Journalism.

In recent times, environmental news and climate change have become more mainstream. And therein lies an opportunity for significant parts of the media to shift from being overly tied to political events, to being more expansive and adaptive in setting future agendas.

Finally, a project like the ICIB may not change things overnight; nevertheless, it is identifying better pathways in dealing with core issues and challenges. It is putting the first brick in an everlasting network for experts and reporters that will work for the water and people, beyond politics.

Reporting on Water Diplomacy: Does Gender Matter?

3

By Jenniver Sehring,[1] Rozemarijn ter Horst[2] and Alexandra Said[3]
[1]*Senior Lecturer in Water Governance and Diplomacy, IHE Delft;* [2]*Lecturer in Water Diplomacy and Cooperation, IHE Delft;* [3]*Programme Officer, Transboundary Water Cooperation, SIWI*

Introduction

What image comes to mind when you think about women and water? Maybe that of women with a water bucket on their head. This is what we often see in the media and reports of aid organizations. It is probably not a picture of female delegation leaders signing a cooperative agreement on shared waters. On these occasions, we usually see men.

In media, donor reports and research articles that address gender and water management, the focus is usually on water supply and sanitation at household level or local management in the agricultural sector. Transboundary water governance, water diplomacy and conflict prevention at an interstate level is seen as a man's world. Indeed, numbers show that women are under-represented in decision-making positions in transboundary river basin organizations. Often, this is not further reflected, as political processes and decisions are assumed to be neutral. However, they are highly gendered, and in this chapter we want to show why and how.

Gendered Practices and Narratives of Water Diplomacy

Water conflict and cooperation at the transboundary level exists at the intersection of two highly masculinized fields: diplomacy and water resources management. By masculinized we mean that it is not only positions mainly held by men, but also that the core ideas, values and guiding principles of these fields are shaped by men and male assumptions.

The earliest known example of diplomacy is the Amarna system (15-13th century BCE) among the kingdoms of Egypt, Mesopotamia, Assyria and other great powers. Its guiding idea was that the great kings formed a brotherhood. They addressed each other as 'my brother', and as brothers they saw each other as of equal status. Throughout history, (imagined) kinship continued to be an important factor in diplomacy and conflict resolution. But these kinships were seen as brothers, not sisters. This is not surprising: it was not before the early 20th century that women were allowed to work in the diplomatic services around the world, and still today the vast majority of ambassadors are men.

The water sector is also shaped by masculinized practices and discourses. Water experts mainly come from engineering disciplines that have been male-dominated. These engineers decide on and plan water supply, construction of dams and allocation of water. This means that water management, policy guidance and decision making across the basin is often done by men, upon the advice of men, and without including the perspectives, needs or values of women, even though women are often the main water stewards and water providers of their communities.

Beyond the lack of women's representation, the practices and narratives of water diplomacy are also gendered. An example is the Aral Sea Basin in Central Asia, where the key water decision makers are almost exclusively men. There, water negotiations often get stuck because of a culture of not giving in. Many observers ascribe this to the concept of 'strongmen': leadership based on personal and authoritarian forms of power that cannot risk being seen as weak. Compromise in water negotiations is seen not as solution but as failure, and cooperation becomes difficult. At the same time, certain urgent water challenges like water release in drought periods or data requirements are effectively addressed at an informal level. A usual justification for this cooperation is the 'brotherly ties' among the riparian countries which require mutual solidarity. Thus, male experts and policy makers are justifying both confrontative and cooperative practices with certain ideas of masculinity – either strongmen or brothers.

How Does this Affect the Potential for Conflict Resolution?

How do these gendered practices in water diplomacy affect the facilitation of cooperation between states and the prevention and resolution of water-related conflict?

First, it matters what and who is seen as being part of the problem and part of the solution. This raises questions such as 'do certain groups experience a higher impact of the ongoing conflict than others?' and 'are their needs considered in the negotiated solution?' Including more perspectives makes a process more complex, but leads to a more comprehensive understanding of the challenges, and therefore to more sustainable solutions to water conflicts. For example, since women are often disproportionally affected by droughts, floods and water scarcity, their experiences should be part of the problem analysis solutions. The discussion on who is affected by a conflict and by the proposed solutions is not only taking place in closed government negotiations, but can be influenced by a broader societal discourse in which journalists and researchers play a role.

Second, it matters who sits at the negotiation table. Lead negotiators are often senior diplomats, supported by a larger team of diplomats and specialists. Whether this group is diverse in terms of gender depends on the culture of a country and within the responsible ministries. Does it matter whether representatives in water negotiations are men or women? The answer is yes. Having a diverse group allows dialogues to be more open for different experiences and viewpoints, which enriches discussions. At the same time, a common perception is that women would be more oriented to peace, eager to find and accept compromise, and adverse towards violence and war – while confrontation, dominance, competition, and war are associated with men. Whether true or not, such stereotypes can affect the dynamics of negotiations.

Women's Role in Water Diplomacy

Let's have a look at two shared river basins and the role women play in water diplomacy.

The Nile Basin

The Nile connects eleven countries, and several platforms have been created at various levels to bring together decision makers and experts from the Basin. While they are not often pictured and quoted in the media, women are working in water diplomacy in the Basin. An example is the Nile Basin Initiative (NBI) Technical Advisory Committee that advises the Nile Council of Ministers in charge of water affairs (Nile-COMS), the highest political and decision-making body of the NBI. This Committee consists of two experts from each of the countries. Out of these 18 experts, six are women. With the aim to increase the visibility of women working in transboundary water management of the Nile, facilitate networking, and develop capacities, the Women in Water Diplomacy in the Nile Network was established in 2017 and is hosted by the Stockholm International Water Institute. With junior, mid-level and senior members, the networks facilitates mentorship and cross-generational learning. So far 43 women from nine Nile Basin states have participated in the annual workshops, and interact through informal platforms. Having a strong network contributes to the advancement of women's careers to higher positions. It can also be a contact point for journalists who wish to include women's perspectives.

The Rhine Basin

The Rhine Basin connects nine countries in Western Europe. In 1950, the International Commission for the Protection of the Rhine (ICPR) was founded and has developed into a comprehensive framework for all joint management issues of the river and for addressing disagreements in a peaceful way. Today, women are the majority in leadership and scientific positions in the ICPR. But this was not always the case. Around 2005 the first woman was appointed as head of a delegation to the ICPR. It is hard to say exactly what the reasons for this were – changes in procedures to hire people in ministries, in ideas on who is responsible for childcare, in professional identities of water experts or diplomats, or other. In our research we have found that women who currently hold leadership positions, or held those in the past, share the feeling that in the beginning of their careers they had to prove themselves more, and work harder, than male colleagues. The changes are experienced as positive; those in a position to compare male-dominated or mixed negotiations prefer to have a mix of men and women as they feel that in a mixed group the changed group dynamics provide more space to discuss each other's needs. With this information, the negotiators can potentially find more solutions that have the support of all parties involved.

Conclusion: Implications for Gender-sensitive Reporting about Water Diplomacy

What does the gendered nature of water diplomacy mean for reporting on water conflicts and water cooperation? Across the world women are increasingly taking up spaces which previously were dominated by men, also in water diplomacy. However, often women are not portrayed as leaders, experts and agents of change, but as victims or vulnerable groups. Gender-sensitive reporting can change this – by representing female decision makers in their professional roles, but also by pointing to their absence – e.g. pointing to all-male delegations or expert panels. Another aspect is to concentrate reporting not only on the (male) leaders, but to show the variety of actors who contribute to any negotiation or agreement – which automatically brings a more diverse picture of the relevant actors. Finally, it is crucial to question seemingly 'neutral', 'usual' and taken-for-granted practices and ask if there wouldn't be alternative ways to address water conflicts if other actors were to be given a voice.

4

The Minister, the Prophet and God's Eye
Scientists' voices in Nile media reporting

By Emanuele Fantini
IHE Delft Institute for Water Education

The coronavirus pandemic has placed scientific facts and research at the center of media coverage, revamping discussions on the role of scientists in the public debate, and on the relation between science and politics. The issues are highly relevant also for media in water conflicts and cooperation, as technical and scientific controversies are often at the core of water disputes between and within states. The negotiations between Egypt, Ethiopia and Sudan on the filling and operation of the Grand Ethiopian Renaissance Dam (GERD) are a good example here.

Communicating science is a difficult job, always needing to find the right balance between accuracy and accessibility. The task can be even more challenging in the context of international water conflicts, where techno-scientific facts and information become sensitive political issues. In these contexts, often the imperatives of national interest and security crush critical analysis and journalists' or researchers' freedom of expression.

This chapter reflects on how scientists' or experts' voices are reported in the coverage of international water conflicts, drawing on a research on Nile media narratives undertaken within the project 'Open Water Diplomacy. Media, science and transboundary cooperation in the Nile basin'. Overall, our analysis of 980 articles published between 2013 and 2018 in 10 media outlets (2 each for Egypt, Sudan, Ethiopia, Uganda and the global media) shows that scientists and scientific research are poorly represented in media coverage of Nile issues.

Numbers and Science

Taking numbers and figures as proxy for the reporting of scientific or technical facts, we found those in 57% of the articles analyzed. However, more than half of these articles made a limited use of numbers and figures, namely featuring only 1 or 2 numbers in the text. Our sample being mainly constructed around events relating to the GERD, the majority of these numbers are related to infrastructure and hydropower: most of the time they refer to the overall budget of the dam project and its completion rate. The fact that the latter remained the same throughout years suggests a simple cut and paste from the internet, but also points at the challenge of getting up to date and reliable information on politically sensitive water projects.

How are these numbers contextualized? We found that only 18% of the articles mentioned a scientific report or study, with the overwhelming majority failing in providing a link to the study or even quoting its title. And whose voices had brought it to discuss technical and scientific facts, or to sketch the broader picture within which the audience should understand these facts? Journalists tended to most frequently quote politicians (in 72% of the articles), followed by government officials, like diplomats or representatives of technical ministries (38% of the articles), and experts and/or scientists (31%).

We were particularly interested in exploring how the latter are represented and used by journalists. In other words, when and how do journalists quote experts and scientists when reporting on Nile issues? Through a critical discourse analysis of our sample, we identified three main characters that are played by experts and scientists in media debates on the Nile: the minister, the prophet, and God's eye. These characters reflect and highlight different attributes and roles that might be assigned to science in the public debate.

The Minister: Preaching the Catechism of National Interest

Identifying and counting the voices quoted in the articles was not a straightforward task. In particular, the distinction between government officials and experts/scientists can be blurred, as the experts that are often interviewed might belong to research centres that are affiliated to national ministries, or might be scholars who are also recruited as technical advisor to their national government, for instance in the tripartite negotiations on the GERD. These experts are often hosted in mainstream and government-controlled media. Most of the time these voices 'explain', and 'argue'. They are mostly national experts, from one of the riparian countries. The data and numbers they present are often unchallenged, as their main purpose is to legitimize specific claims and official government discourses on the sharing and management of Nile waters. In this case, scientific data and expertise tell the (official) truth and represent the 'facts', often as opposed to 'opinion' or 'emotions'. In a few interesting cases, the claims of such embedded experts are confronted with those of their homologues from other riparian countries, to illustrate the different positions at the negotiation table. This allows journalists and their audiences to reflect on the complexities of science and to take a more critical stance towards the use of techno-scientific data to legitimize political agendas.

The Prophet: Warning About Future Crisis and Concern

Interviews with experts and scientists can be also used to introduce new or different topics. In this case the scientist 'points at', or 'warns about' key issues that are missing or that might be overlooked in the public debate or in diplomatic negotiations. Such a voice can be considered that of an (unheard) prophet, as it often presents future scenarios, pointing for instance at population growth, pollution, unsustainable consumptions, and climate change implications for water resources and management. Such a list of topics suggests that these prophets often play the role of the doomsayer. The scenarios they depict are rather gloomy and mostly framed in terms of 'crisis'. These experts are both local and international. Here the scientist is perceived as someone that can see something that the layperson does not see. Scientific facts also allow the introduction of a different time scale, looking at the long-term implications of water management, and contrasting the more short-term views of political or economic interests. Thus scientific data and technical expertise can be used to point at the narrowness of the public debate and to foreground issues that should be taken up in the political and diplomatic agenda.

God's Eye View: Suggesting Pathways for Conflict Mediation and Resolution

Journalists might also evoke scientists and technical knowledge to bring in a solution to the water problem they are investigating. Most of the time such solutions come from outside the political boundaries of the controversy; they are illustrated through the voice of international scholars or by quoting international studies or research groups. An archetypal example is the lawyer from a third country commenting on the principles and norms of international law that should be applied to negotiate and mediate the conflict. A second example is the reference to and the display of remote sensing and satellite images, conveying the idea of a neutral and impartial representation of the physical word. In both cases technical and scientific knowledge come from above, with a sort of God's eye view allowing the identification of key principles and judgement on the legitimacy of diplomatic positions, or the ability to measure water uses and evaluate the water productivity of crops, fields and countries. Here science is represented as independent and neutral, above the parties (sometimes literally, like in the case of remote sensing). Scientific data and technical expertise are brought in to provide independent and reliable data and information, to suggest pathways for conflict mediation and resolutions, with the assumption that it should inspire decision making.

Plurality is Key

These three characters are neither exclusive nor exhaustive. All of them can be interesting and worth being represented. They might coexist in the same article or even in the same scientist. By pointing at these three stereotypes, we want to elicit a double reflection: journalists should think about their views on science and its role in society, and perhaps be more explicit about it; scientists could plan more systematically why and how to engage in the public debate and consider this as an inherent part of their job. Throughout the project 'Open Water Diplomacy', we learnt that a better conversation and closer collaboration between journalists and scientists can be fostered by acknowledging that these two groups share the goal of representing reality in a way that is accurate and trustworthy.

The idea of plurality seems key to working towards this goal. First, media coverage of Nile issues should reflect the plurality and the debates within and between sciences: this could be done by giving voice to more than one discipline – not only technical or legal – to explore the different dimensions of the problem and its complexity. Second, a plurality of tools – maps, infographic and data visualization – can facilitate the communication of such technical and complex information, as shown in several reportages on the Nile published in the first months of 2020, when the negotiations on the GERD hit the headlines of global media. Third, as water science and water diplomacy remain a rather masculine environment, we urge journalists to foreground voices of women scientists, thinking of them as a role model rather than the exception that makes the news. Finally, even if in this article, and often in our research we have been using 'experts' and 'scientists' almost as synonyms, we recognize that there are different kinds of expertise and knowledge that can contribute to identify problems and solutions: farmers, indigenous people, water users are often portrayed and quoted as victims of global water crisis beyond their control. Thinking about these people in terms of experts might foreground original experiences and creative solutions to navigate water problems, and it will better reflect the plurality of ways of knowing, understanding and representing water.

Covering Water in Times of Conflict

By Ayah Aman
Al-Shorouk Egyptian Daily Newspaper

Fig. 5.1. Nile Falls near Lake Tana, Ethiopia. Photo by Michael Tsegay.

The Nile has always been a great source of inspiration to writers, poets and artists, featuring its water, charm and people. Journalists even take it one step further, exploring a little more beyond what is clearly seen, to what is true. They follow its path, unravelling live stories, highlighting lives revolving around the river, power dynamics, conflicts of interest and much more. This obviously doesn't come without a price.

The Nile is a river shared by 11 countries, and is always perceived as a source of prosperity and economic development, where the river is the source for food and energy security. While the Nile has a rich history and unique geography and hydrology, it is rather complex to cover, especially when it comes to covering conflicts.

Most research *identify* media as a reflection of people's pulse, highlighting their needs and fears, or a platform that facilitates dialogue and cooperation, yet it can also be seen as a tool to incite conflicts over water.

Water diplomacy can be divided into nine categories (government, professional conflict resolution, business, funding, religion, research and education, activism and private citizen). Media also comes as an important element as it plays a crucial role in shaping the public opinion.

Nile and Media Coverage: Overview

Stories about the Nile on both local and regional levels are always there, but it is how the media handles the story that makes all the difference – whether as an opportunity for collaboration or conflict.

Taking a quick look at the local media covering Nile Basin countries, we can easily see the prevalence of local perspectives; most reports, articles, breaking news and even photos focus on national interests. It mostly shows how the Nile is a vital source for the country and the people's needs. But with the continuous change in the Nile hydropolitics (mainly after the signing of the Cooperative Framework Agreement (CFA) in 2010, and the construction of the Grand Ethiopian Renaissance Dam (GERD) in 2011), the media coverage turned to have a more regional perspective, looking more into activities in the riparian countries, exploring how their possible impacts on the national interest might look.

For instance, if we look into media coverage in Eastern Nile countries, we would find that stories written about the Nile mostly revolve around disciplines of security, conflict, international relations, and only recently some attention has been given to environmental aspects. While identity is a vital narrative, there are also many other essential aspects to investigate here.

In Egypt for example, media usually put it this way: the Nile is a critical source for the Egyptian people, a matter of life or death. Similarly, in Ethiopia, after the construction of the GERD, the Nile was being framed as a national issue and GERD has been discussed from the national perspective. Positive perspectives that promote cooperation were also there, but only during times of political understanding like signing the DOP in 2015 (a declaration that defines the cooperation between Egypt, Sudan and Ethiopia on GERD filling and operations, and the principles of peaceful settlement of disputes).

Challenges and Mitigation

Media in the Nile Basin has the potential to establish a constructive dialogue and show updates about the continuous changes taking place in the Basin. Media also has the capacity to help raise the general public's understanding and influence decision-making processes. Nevertheless, it can also do exactly the opposite.

I perceive balance, objectivity, responsibility and credibility as essential for any media coverage. Out of my experience, the following are common challenges that face almost all journalists writing about water.

Fig. 5.2. Kids diving in the River Nile in Qanater, Egypt. Photo by Roger Anis.

- **Understanding the technical, political, legal and social aspects of the water conflict.**

Ultimately, journalists need sound knowledge to be able to tackle the issue and deliver it in a simple way to the audience. The best solution is to build this knowledge, through keeping all necessary information and data, keeping track of the latest research and scientific articles, and always being on top of new research, news and analyses. This should be done in parallel with establishing sound relations with scientists, officials and relevant institutes.

- **Credible sources**

Writing about water can be very sensitive; this is especially true during events like negotiations over controversial issues. Sometimes the journalist is being obligated to keep most of the information anonymous, which interferes with

his/her credibility. This should be essentially accompanied by publishing trustworthy information from credible sources.
- **Lack of confidence**

In many cases, the media is viewed with doubt: by the government, experts and the public. This is mainly due to negative stereotypes on media impacts during negotiation periods. The role of the journalist here, although hard, is not impossible, and each journalist can build his/her own credibility, while always being careful about how he/she writes and presents facts.
- **Non-regular coverage**

Nile or water issues are more of a seasonal issue, covered when there is a new update, such as meetings, visits, negotiations, project inaugurations, etc.

So, journalists should be aware of this and keep covering water creatively, exposing different dimensions and interests, not only those that are concerned with the news. Following relevant scientific updates might work for a good source of topics when journalists run out of ideas.

Solutions for Constructive Media Coverage on the Nile

Helping the media to do its job in Nile coverage no doubt needs good understanding and collaboration among all stakeholders: the government, experts, researchers and involved institutions.

Some international institutions like the Nile Basin Initiative (NBI), Stockholm International Water Institute (SIWI), IHE Delft Institute for Water Education, International Water Management Institute (IWMI) and German Corporation for International Cooperation (GIZ) had realised the significant role played by the media in water diplomacy; this has in turn created sound expertise in enhancing and boosting water reporting in recent years. This has been possible through the training of specialized journalists, conducting constructive dialogues, enhancing media coverage in the Nile Basin, and linking journalists with researchers and officials in workshops to discuss the best solutions for informative and positive coverage.

- **Raising awareness**

On July 28, 2016, a group of 26 journalists from Ethiopia, Egypt and Sudan participated in five days of training in Addis Ababa, Assosa (capital of the Beninshangul regional state) and at the site of GERD itself. The training was organized by SIWI under the UNDP Shared Waters Partnership. It was the first time that such a big media delegation, especially from Egypt, had visit GERD. Through the training, there was a constructive dialogue on political, technical, legal and economic aspects of the cooperation climate in the Eastern Nile Basin region.

'My perspective has significantly changed. Now I can understand how others within the Nile basin think about us' explains Bassem Abass, an Egyptian journalist who had participated in the SIWI workshop and other workshops conducted by NBI, SIWI and IHE.

Abbas highlights: 'Through workshops, I had the opportunity to learn more about the conditions of other Nile countries, through discussions and views exchanged with other journalists.'

- **Keeping journalists well informed**

Abbas contends, 'After the GERD field visit, I felt scientifically enlightened, I got the information directly from the site, not from officials who haven't visited the dam; I had an advantage.'

After the training, Abbas published an article that won the 2017 Nile Media Award – at Ahram online (state media) website, speaking on the aspiration of Ethiopian people and their willingness to build the dam.

Abbas affirmed: 'Not only workshops could help in balanced and objective coverage, but the awareness of the journalist himself/herself.'

Fig. 5.3. A Sudanese young man having coffee by the Nile at sunrise, Sudan. Photo by Ahmed Saeed.

- **Building networks among journalists and experts**

Conducting workshops for journalists will definitely help in building networks among journalists from all Nile riparian countries, along with experts, officials and involved institutions, and sustain those links via social media groups. These groups gained good experience in communication ready for big events involving negotiations, sharing information, opinions and analyses.

These networks help in times of conflict as they give journalists the chance to understand the other part of the story, and allow them access to official statements that are sometimes published in local languages.

My own experience includes the opportunity, as a journalist from Egypt, to meet with Solomon Goshu, a journalist from Ethiopia, and to share experiences on main media challenges in the Nile Basin, and tricks for positive coverage. This understanding comes after many events, discussions and field visits I had with Goshu in Ethiopia, Sudan and Egypt. One of the best practices I would share is to work in the field with a colleague from another background, as this will open your eyes to the other part of the story.

- **Telling the other part of the story**

Another successful experience was #EverydayNile, a project conducted by Roger Anis, an Egyptian photojournalist. The project came after a workshop on media and water diplomacy by IHE in the Netherlands. Through the project, Anis sought to convey a visual image of people's relationship with water, for better understanding among different populations sharing the Nile blessings.

In ten days, travelling through Ethiopia, Anis had excellent shots. 'I was shocked that people who live beside the source of the Nile, don't have access to clean water, and drink directly from Lake Tana, or fill their jerry cans.'

Photographs have special power in times of conflict, which is another value added. Anis comments, 'Images can be really appealing and efficient to inform people, especially on social media.' He believes that from a visual point of view, simple and direct information is always better.

The fact that there are some successful experiences here or there, does not mean there is a radical change in favor of reducing conflicts. Nevertheless, we can still count on journalists' increased awareness, and endeavors of specialized institutes in promoting better understanding among considerable segments of journalists covering the Nile.

Water Reporting
Beyond dry pieces, nurture your coverage

By Elzahraa Jadallah
Writer and freelance journalist

Fig. 6.1. Sudanese man selling water in the outskirts of Omdurman city. Photo by the author.

When I first started working on water reporting a few years ago, I thought then that water is such a limited topic, and wondered how I would get enough ideas for ongoing stories; I thought I would run out of fresh stories by the end of the first year at best.

Practising water reporting, however, turned out to be exactly the opposite: flowing and vibrant, something similar to the river Nile I am covering, an endless source of wonders. I found water running through many interesting and diverse topics, and very much connected to society and economy and people's daily lives.

Looking at water from that new perspective opened my eyes to see how it is interwoven in almost every topic that deals with the basic needs of communities – Sustainable Development Goals (SDGs), transboundary cooperation, water management, scarcity, hygiene, pollution, dams, are just drops in an ocean for topics that can be produced in this respect.

Water investigative work can also be a rich field, where journalists can cover in-depth issues such as pollution, water projects, dams, water conflicts, among others. In-depth reporting gains its charm from its ability to reflect various sides of the story, reveal what is hidden, and possibly incur real change on the ground.

Reporting Sensitive Water Issues

When you start writing a story, divide it into stages. For me, I split it into three: research phase, field work and desk work. Although the amount of work and preparation differ according to the type of story, angle of coverage and contacts needed, overall keep the following tips in consideration:

- Study your topic thoroughly, collect key scientific findings from credible sources, as well as information about the field you'll be visiting later.
- Based on your research, make a list of contacts, and start communicating with them as soon as possible, to set up interviews. Time here is strategic, setting up interviews early will give you time for other experts, if the selected ones turn out to be busy or reject your request.
- Learn about the nature of the place you are writing about, the culture of the people, the environment and risks associated with the work you aim to do. Understanding the context and the settings is crucial to stay safe while reporting sensitive issues. You can then comply with cultural norms for the place you intend to cover, especially for females, taking into account how to dress and if you need to take a male colleague while going there. For instance, in many cases, it would be wise to wear a headscarf while working in rural areas, rather than jeans and a T-shirt which is fine in the capital.
- Set a budget that you can abide by. In this case, you should write down all expected expenses for your field work, including travel, accommodation, pocket money, etc. This part will have more significance if you are applying for a grant to cover your story, and it is usually sent along with the story pitch.
- Set a realistic schedule, so you can meet the deadline, without being overstressed.
- Always keep your editor updated on your progress, and ask for more time if needed.

Field Work

Fig. 6.2. Sudanese woman getting water from a public tank due to lack of proper supply, Omdurman, 2018. Photo by the author.

This part is crucial to the story structure and final shape. Sometimes describing the settings where the story takes place, it is the master scene that cannot be skipped. This does not always happen, yet, it is always essential, as this would be the main link between the people and the story.

- Set a clear plan for your logistics.
- Establish a network of reliable sources from the area to help (help you stay safe and move around).
- If you feel there is risk, keep a low profile.
- Avoid any unnecessary movements.
- Be careful when recording statements, make sure your device is working well.
- Document all your findings and write notes about the place and the people and all your insights.
- Write down the interviews you conducted as soon as you can, while words are still there in your mind, even if you have recorded them or taken notes.

Desk Work

Coming back from the field, you are one step from accomplishing the mission, you now have a better idea of the context, and you are about to compile field work and research together.

- Now, do further research and restructure your story if needed.
- Conduct more interviews, perhaps with scientists, after you have already had some interviews with the people. For better results, show your credibility to your sources, through recording their input and carefully taking

notes. You can also send them the article before publishing – you can always get their answers through email, to eliminate any chance of misquoting. Explain to scientists how their contribution will influence people's awareness, and to officials, the impact of their statement in fighting rumours.
- Keep in mind to build your network of scientists, officials and colleagues, through repeated and sustainable engagement with individuals and institutes.

It's also important to establish good relations with your fellow journalists. They can be crucial while working on transboundary stories, as you would normally need someone to advise you about sources in other countries, or they could even do some field work, so that you write the article together. Collaborative stories are greatly welcomed by regional and international platforms.

Before sending the story to your editor, you might want to:

- Get back to your sources, in case you have missed anything in the interview, or you need more information or clarification.
- Rewrite, edit and proofread your story carefully, before sending it to the editor, so that it is easily comprehended and what you want to say flows smoothly.
- Always ask yourself: how you could make your article different from similar ones out there – a new angle? New scientific facts? Significant interviewees? Illustrations?
- Keep in mind to maintain gender balance for your interviewees, and the balance of voices represented throughout the article – always keep it fair.

Good planning and hard work are fundamental to producing in-depth coverage; nevertheless, there are always some challenges throughout the process.

Challenges and Mitigation

- You might be denied access to information or sources: try other sources/individuals/institutes. For instance, if you have been rejected by an official/governmental body, approach other scientific institutes that are equally credible.
- Normally, your interviewees are busy people. There there is a high possibility that they will ignore your request or send you delayed responses. Here, you should be aware that this is normal, and then work out your way to get them committed. There is no one size fits all, some will respond to multiple reminders, others might rather respond through reminding them of their input's significance, etc.
- What might be a constant challenge is the difficulty of scientific research and the terminology included. Read through the paper several times, and identify parts/issues that you cannot get. You can then contact the author, or an expert, to get a better understanding, after which, break it into small pieces, in simple points that convey the message to unspecialized readers.
- Lack of funding is a significant hurdle in water stories, especially if you are a freelance journalist, yet you can still apply for funds and get them, if you learn how to pitch your stories properly. This needs thorough research of similar stories, so as to produce a novel and interesting angle and approach

to the story. Also, when you succeed in getting a grant, impress your employer, and your reputation will get you more chances in the future.

Fig.6.3. A farmer in Tuti Island in Khartoum is checking his old manual pump before using it to get water from the Nile, 2019. Photo by the author.

Conclusion

It is unfortunate that science stories in general have fewer readers and less interest on news portals, yet if you write a good story, it will find its way to the publisher. The question is, what does a good story look like?

Here are few tips, to help give you a good story:

- Data and language should be simple and clear.
- Keep the story short and to the point, don't lose your reader.
- Use photos, multi-media (videos, interactive maps, graphs, charts, etc.) in online stories and sound effects in radio. Be creative!
- Make your story relevant to the readers, especially when you report about communities; don't ever forget the human angle throughout the story.
- Use credible sources and provide evidence.
- Rely on facts, demonstrated by research and information from reliable sources in addition to your own observations. Avoid including rumours or reporting pseudoscience.
- Make sure you understand what you are writing about. Don't contribute to the ever-growing problem of misinformation.
- When reflecting people's stories, you should be inclusive of citizens of different genders, ages and socio-economic classes, who are all impacted by the same issue.
- Don't rush, take your time to verify your facts and to develop your story.

7

Reporting Shared Narratives
Establishing transboundary cooperation through media

By Fredrick Mugira
Water Journalists Africa

Fig. 7.1. River Nile at Jinja in Uganda. Photograph owned by author.

This chapter addresses an often overlooked area in water diplomacy: the role of journalists in ensuring transboundary cooperation in shared rivers, shaping perceptions and contributing to define the scope of water debates and negotiations.

Africa's river basins are some of the world's most biodiverse regions. River basins provide a key resource for drinking water, fisheries production, navigation, recreation and ecosystem maintenance among other purposes. However, their ecosystems are under threat, not only from population pressure, climate change, pollution and dams, but also from conflicts and lack of cooperation among riparian nations.

Many water diplomats are working to promote cooperation among riparian nations, and journalists have a duty to complement their work, through communicating water issues in a way that facilitates water diplomacy, and promotes shared narratives on the river basins of Africa.

But, despite this growing interest in water diplomacy, it is generally ignored by African media. In Burundi for example 'Best sellers are stories on insecurity, stories on core water issues come later', narrates prominent Burundi journalist, Apollinaire Niyirora.

Reasons behind this phenomenon are multiple, most important of which are:

- Competition with sensational stories, those cheap to cover that are also appealing.
- The focus on marketing that is normally translated into covering topics of interest to the segment that would buy, leaving out stories of the rural, poor and marginalized.
- Lack of exposure/awareness of African journalists and editors to concepts of environmental conservation and similar concerns.
- Complex, boring and dry nature of some environmental issues that are usually multi-dimensional.
- Government control of the media in some African countries, thus journalists have no say on what to cover. In other African countries, water issues are only covered as a national security issue.

In Ethiopia for example, Salem Mulugeta, a prominent Ethiopian journalist, says 'Most of the issues related to water development are seen as sensitive, so access to such information is very limited.'

Communicating Water Issues to National and International Audiences

Amid this era of unprecedented access to information, it is of utmost significance that journalists rely on, and in turn publish, credible information that states facts and trustworthy data. As a water journalist myself, I suggest that journalists take the following tips into consideration.

Regional significance

Include a regional significance in your story and write responsibly on common interests for the whole region, involving only credible resources. Write, expose and explain transnational issues in ways that make more sense to all residents of the river basin, thus inviting regional reaction and participation.

Minimize harm

Always consider possible consequences of your stories and interviews, so to avert any harm to officials, researchers, scientists and even people who volunteered to share their experiences through their stories. This does not mean, however, that you should act in a paranoid way, after all we are in search of the truth – just find better ways to present your information in the safest way.

Respect history, culture and people

Always respect the river basin's history, culture, and people. Also, beware that river basins' landscapes are continuously changing; always keep on top of any updates. River basin journalism cannot be taken out of the socio-economic, cultural, political and environmental contexts. Use local journalists and media to get local sources that can give you more vivid perspectives and views.

Give them a voice

Give the people the chance to tell their stories: this will help in building trust. It will serve two purposes: on the one hand, you will be informing the public and raising their awareness on issues that directly affect their daily lives, and on the other hand, your narratives will have a human dimension that is the true essence of storytelling. Also, let them contribute to disseminating information. This can be through providing ways for citizens to submit stories online, over WhatsApp or calling on the radio. This will provide excellent outreach.

Welcome criticism

Be constructive and accept criticism when raised; it is a two-sided relationship, and as we journalists do criticize some researchers, scientists, officials or institutes, we should also accept the opposite. Journalists and media institutions that hold officials, researchers and scientists accountable, should themselves display qualities of transparency expected by such professionals and accept scrutiny.

Fig. 7.2. The view of the Nile in Cairo. Photograph owned by author.

Improving Interaction Between Journalists and Officials

Close the trust gap

Many scientists and officials argue that they never trust journalists because they often misrepresent facts and statements.

This is in fact true for some journalists, and it really needs to be put in focus: it is paramount that writers and editors find, crosscheck and present scientific facts simply and clearly. Always question the accuracy and credibility of the information, especially figures and statistics. Your duty as a journalist is to report the truth. Make sure the information in your story is true, correct, exact and free from any errors or mistakes.

Be careful with how you deliver the content, and make use of photography and other multimedia products, such as maps and videos. These tools essentially offer perspective, add tone and provide an accurate representation of facts.

Talk to scientists to get a deeper knowledge of the science behind the topic you are covering, record their input, or get their response through email, so as to prevent any misquoting.

You should be very careful while putting together your questions, they should be comprehensive, covering all aspects of a given topic. And if the topic is widely covered by different media outlets, figure out an innovative angle of coverage.

Wanjohi Kabukuru, prominent Kenyan journalist notes, 'Many journalists would approach researchers, asking off-the-cuff questions and get general answers, at the time they can get very valuable and in-depth information.'

Beware of the difference between opinions and facts, always be careful how you use words and place important facts, or else you may end up sending the wrong signals or giving the wrong impressions. And most importantly, refrain from using inaccurate information just to spur interest in your story or get more traffic. Leave sensation to advertisers.

Build relations

Exert some effort to find relevant scientists, researchers and officials working in your river basin, and start building relationships with them. Pick trustworthy and qualified personnel, with no hidden agendas, and once you have found the right candidates, stay in touch and make your relationship sustainable.

Always bear in mind the safety of your sources, especially while reporting sensitive issues. Keep in mind that your role as a journalist goes beyond just reporting.

Coproduce knowledge

Writing on technical and scientific issues is key in shaping public debate and orienting international negotiations on transboundary waters, but scientists' and journalists' work remains, on many occasions, isolated or blindly expressing national perspectives. But this can be addressed by bringing together journalists and scientists, to create content, both online and offline, via user-friendly platforms such as infoamazonia.org, which provides news and reports of the endangered Amazon region; sciDev.Net, a source of news, views and analysis about science and technology globally; https://infonile.org/en/, a geojournalism project focused on the Nile Basin; or theconversation.com, which publishes news stories written by academics and researchers.

Co-production of knowledge, which involves discussions and information sharing among scientists and journalists could also help to build trust between the two parties.

InfoNile

Fig. 7.3. This marker in the River Nile, in Jinja, Uganda, indicates the exact point where the Nile starts. Photograph owned by author.

A good example of balanced water coverage is InfoNile.org that was founded in 2017, with support from IHE Delft, as a project of Water Journalists Africa, a 700+ member network of water journalists across the African continent. It is a geojournalism platform that combines interactive maps with stories, to promote local data journalism on topics related to water and the environment in the the Nile Basin. It is a cross-border media organization with a network of about 400 water journalists, across the 11 Nile Basin countries, reporting for print, TV, radio and online platforms.

InfoNile is bridging gaps between Nile Basin scientists, researchers, journalists and the general public, to increase mutual awareness and understanding of the various dimensions of covering water. It challenges chauvinistic and nationalistic perspectives on the use of Nile waters, through facilitating joint work and co-production of knowledge. Through training and grants, InfoNile enhances Nile journalists' and scientists' communicative and collaborative skills, building their capacities to provide accurate and holistic information on water politics, along with social and environmental issues. It is also a useful resource for students and researchers, as it provides data visualizations, videos, digital mapping, audio podcasts, in-depth multimedia stories and more.

In addition to researchers and students, InfoNile further communicates scientific information and data on water issues to officials, NGOs, policymakers, etc.

Media and Water, is the Glass Half Full?

By Rehab Abdelmohsen
Freelance journalist

Fig. 8.1. A view of the Nile in Aswan, upper Egypt. Photo by the author.

While I was interviewing an expert regarding water scarcity in the Middle East, she told me a quote that I would never forget. She said, 'Whiskey is for drinking, water is for fighting'!

This statement gives you a glimpse of how water conflicts are attractive for both editors and readers; it is an excellent hook and the perfect subject to spice up a story about transboundary waters – however, the fact we cannot ignore is that water can really work as a ground for cooperation.

Resisting the attraction of linking water to war is not easy for journalists, and to avoid falling into this trap, I always try to ask myself what are the missing details in a given story? Is the available information making sense? It is always useful to be critical and to thoroughly explore the subject from different angles, be it a press release or a research paper.

In 2019, I had the chance to attend the workshop 'Media, Science, and Water: Telling the story of the Nile' at IHE DELFT, Netherlands, and during a lecture on water diplomacy, Rozemarijn ter Horst talked about a well-known research paper 'Water, Drought, Climate Change, and Conflict in Syria' published by Peter H. Gleick in 2014.

Through her study, Ter Horst noticed that media bias towards covering the scenario of droughts and war is very obvious; she explained that there was a journalist who kept calling her, asking for a comment on the topic of the water conflict. But when she started talking about water as a source of harmony, and how the water dispute could lead to positive outcomes and encourage dialogues to reach compromise, the journalist repeated his question and said: 'What about conflicts over water?'

Doubt. Read. Ask

While reporting scientific research, many media outlets make researchers sound 100% certain about the results, which is exactly the opposite of the nature of scientific studies. Researchers are always open to endless possibilities; for instance, new research could prove the opposite, invalidating the original – and this is what actually happened with Dr Gleick's research.

Dealing with research as fact should not be our approach as water journalists, but rather it should be dealt with as information that must be questioned and further researched. To be able to do so, it is always advisable to *avoid single-source stories*, no matter how tempting. You should get views from other scientists, and study the evidence presented by the researcher carefully. With practice, you will find that some research is scientifically flawed and some is based on hidden agendas.

Before going to your resources, it is always important to *do your work and*, read thoroughly about the topic. For example, if you are covering water treatment, it is better to know the difference between blue, green and grey water; if you cover water in Sudan, you have to know the number of rivers in the country, what kind of problems they face, how much has been achieved, and so forth.

Avoid Misleading the People Who Trusted You

If you are covering transboundary rivers, then you are into a very sensitive subject, and a single wrong word could change the whole meaning. I remember how misquoting an expert working for the Ministry of Water Resources and Irrigation in Egypt caused a series of consequences, one of which was dismissing him from work, and preventing other experts from speaking to the media.

This is why *recording the interview* is a necessity, first to get the quotes accurately, and second to have it documented, in case the expert himself/herself forgot or got confused about what was said. Sometimes it is better to *send the quotes to the source again to double check*.

During the interview, remember *there is no such a thing as a stupid question*; never feel shy to ask your source what they mean by this or that. If you didn't understand it, there is no way that your readers will.

In one of my stories, I was interviewing an expert who said something about wetlands, and he made it sound like a very common word, and although I knew marshlands – one type of wetland – I decided to overcome my shyness and I asked: what are wetlands? And I ended up writing 3 interesting stories on this vital and critical part of our natural environment.

One, Two, a Story to Go

Fig. 8.2. Local worker from Ethiopia removing water hyacinth from the Tana River. Photo by the author.

Writing a story is not one easy straightforward step, it is a process that normally starts with finding a story, with an appealing idea, that fits the platform you are writing for, and then pitching it to the editor.

To find a story, an interesting one, with a new angle, journalists need to be resourceful and attend relevant events related to water. They should then closely follow up news and analyses, especially in local media, while simultaneously keeping an eye on international organizations and subscribing to their mailing lists – and, most importantly, talking informally to experts, they know best, *casual chat led me to story ideas in 90% of cases.*

I also visit science-related websites, such as: sciencenews.org, phys.org, sciencedaily.com, etc. and I also *check water-related scientific journals,* for example: *Applied Water Science, Water Research,* among others.

After this, a journalist needs to *justify to the editor: why should we cover this story?* Here, if you are a freelance journalist, you need to check if this media platform has covered this story before, you need to scan their archive, especially the one related to water, and to have an idea on what are the stories that normally get them hooked.

Next step, send your email and include a clear and concise top line that sums up the story, followed by a few phrases to illustrate the context and background, and then a brief summary of how you plan to cover this story.

Teamwork

Writing about the River Nile is actually charming, yet challenging. It puts all your knowledge and practice to a difficult test, starting from finding a new idea, then reaching an expert who is willing to give comments, and making a real balance by bringing together all the voices from the different countries and diverse views, and seeking balance and objectivity while writing the story.

A good example to give here is two stories I have written about the Grand Ethiopian Renaissance Dam (GERD). The first was in 2013. I remember that back then it was quite easy to find an Egyptian expert to talk to about the topic, but in order to make a balance and to bring the Ethiopian voice to my story, I went through a long process to find one.

Finally, with the help of social media, I got the input of two experts from Ethiopia. I was even blessed that one of them was supportive to the dam and talked about its significance to the public, and the other had some concerns about the environmental effects of the project. Similarly, I got different opinions from the Egyptian experts I quoted, and I had also managed to get a comment from an independent expert at the Stockholm International Water Institute (SIWI); that was a cherry on top.

On the other hand, the second experience wasn't that fortunate. It was in 2020, I noticed how the situation had changed, experts from both countries were dismissive of the idea of media interviews, after many attempts; two experts from Egypt talked to me, but seven experts from Ethiopia refused to give any comments, and again to make a balance, I talked to two researchers from universities in the UK and Sweden.

Does this mean that I did my job? Maybe yes, maybe no. I was talking to an editor about the work I am doing while covering the Nile, and he told me that his correspondent in Ethiopia could not get any comments from the Egyptian experts. At that point, I realized how team work really matters, and that we can do it together, I and my colleagues from other countries.

This is how I got to interview the Sudanese Minister of Water and Irrigation, Yasser Abbas, with the help of a Sudanese colleague. Always remember that networking and communicating with colleagues from different countries is a valuable investment, both on the personal and professional level.

Satisfy People's Thirst for Information
SIWI experience in training water journalists

By Kerry Schneider
Stockholm International Water Institute (SIWI)

Fig 9.1. Journalists from Sudan, South Sudan and Egypt. Photo by the author.

Covering the story of Nile cooperation over the past decade has been no simple task. Setting aside the sensitive political nature of these stories, a Nile journalist must understand, process, and communicate incredibly complex information, such as the drivers of climate and its changes and how those changes affect water availability in time and space. They must oversee the geopolitical situation and related socio-economic drivers that impact how international development interacts with foreign policy.

In order to paint the clearest picture of the cooperation process with balance and impartiality, a journalist must at once be part hydrologist, part economist, part political scientist, part international water law expert, part historian, and the list goes on. If we reintroduce the political dynamics, a journalist in the Nile needs a network, or at least access to government officials who are engaged in policy setting at both national and regional levels.

Journalists must understand that while many water problems have technical solutions they don't exist in a political vacuum and the decision-making processes over major shared water resources like the Nile include numerous ministries or agencies with differing views, mandates, and interests, often in competition with each other. What educational programme in the world could prepare a young reporter for what will be expected of them if they are tasked with following the story of Nile cooperation? How many hats can one wear?

Digesting and Dealing with the Ever-evolving Media Scene

A journalist in the Nile should be always on top of rapidly changing landscapes of how and where media is produced and circulated. Social media has been a game changer, with upsides and downsides, for journalists to promote their stories. While major news outlets have quietly shuttered foreign correspondence offices, limited printed publications, and downscaled in numerous other ways, there is a growing number of news outlets that exist entirely online and often engage freelance journalists from around the world to produce content.

At its base level, the extended reach afforded by these new media outlets and platforms for sharing has meant an increase in opportunity for journalists to work with or for numerous organizations and a story going 'viral' means there is a potential to reach people around the world who may never pick up a copy of a local or national newspaper.

However, the sheer number of places one can access news can make it difficult to filter sound reporting from 'click bait' journalism that is geared towards attracting readership through salacious or controversial headlines, for the purpose of attracting advertisers primarily concerned with the number of times people access a website.

Since 2016, the Stockholm International Water Institute (SIWI) has been trying to fill these gaps by supporting journalists from the Eastern Nile countries (Sudan, South Sudan, Ethiopia, Egypt) who regularly report on Nile issues related to the environment, politics, and major development initiatives such as the Grand Ethiopian Renaissance Dam (GERD). The ambition has been to facilitate a workshop in each of the countries so that journalists have an opportunity to travel and engage other journalists or stakeholders in Nile cooperation across borders. In general, this training has been organized around four primary components.

Encouraging and Strengthening Science-based Reporting

Politics and environmental science are distinctly separate fields and while an article about a water resource investment project for a national or local newspaper may not demand an engineering degree to understand the basic elements, a journalist must still have some level of conceptual understanding appropriate for their readership.

As technical innovations, changes in political economies and hydrological or meteorological realities all drive change from one region to another, journalists must maintain a high level of awareness of these changes in order to accurately reflect on their importance to the general public or decision makers who consume their reporting.

To achieve this, journalists must have greater access to cutting-edge knowledge/information based on established scientific principles and methodologies. They must also have access to the scientists (both national and international) who represent the most direct linkage to informed thinking, as well as politicians or decision makers, in order to communicate the ambitions, status and implications of the political processes surrounding cooperation.

Providing journalists with sufficient resources and opportunities to engage the key individuals involved in transboundary water decision-making processes, enables them to write balanced stories based on facts as opposed to stories revolving around polarizing uninformed speculation that can fuel tension and conflict. In each workshop facilitated by SIWI, experts, from within the Nile region, as well as internationally, have worked with journalists to strengthen their understanding of a wide range of complex issues and to help the journalists contextualize and adapt this information appropriately for outreach to the general public.

Field Visits

In 2016, SIWI organized a field visit to the GERD. This occasion marked the first opportunity for journalists from outside Ethiopia to see the site with their own eyes. Journalists were able to interview focal points involved in the construction process such as government representatives from Ethiopia, take their own photos, etc. There are obvious benefits to providing this in-depth access to journalists, but this visit also took place at a critical time when regional meteorological forecasts suggested that the upcoming rainy season, which annually feeds the Nile, would produce much less precipitation than usual. In such a situation, there is a major risk for downstream countries to perceive reduced river flows as attributed to an upstream countries' withholding of water.

Within the first three months of the workshop's conclusion, over 50 articles or news publications were reported by the participating journalists. A number of high-level government officials, academicians, and other stakeholders closely following the cooperation process provided anecdotal observations that there was a noticeable positive change in the tone and tenor of the news surrounding the GERD's construction. This example demonstrably illustrated the potential of supporting journalists to have immediate short-term impacts in a targeted way while contributing to the broader efforts of improving the quality and balance of reporting on Nile cooperation over the long term.

Enhancing Journalism in an Evolving Media Landscape

An effective journalist following Nile cooperation must have insights into a number of different disciplines but they must also continually develop as writers and as advocates for reporting all of the topics the general public should better understand behind the cooperation process. Through this component, SIWI seeks to strengthen journalists' engagement with the general public as well as their engagement with the traditional structures of media publishers. Topics have included making efficient use of new social media platforms for distribution, honing a story pitch for freelance reporters, or working with editors who may not share the same understanding of all critical but disparate issues embedded in Nile cooperation.

Despite the rapid evolution of social media as a primary source of news for many people around the world, traditional media outlets continue to play an important role in shaping public opinion. However, a journalist in 2020 must make efficient use of social media platforms in order to develop and expand their readership and establish credibility in new or different markets.

In order to strengthen the approach of journalists who must satisfy editors or producers, SIWI has strived to engage other international journalists or media experts who can share their experiences in developing a story pitch or in communicating what elements of a story are of critical importance, so that an editor knows where to focus their efforts.

Creating a Critical Mass of Journalism Excellence Through Collaboration

In transboundary water contexts, in the Nile and elsewhere, upstream developments are often perceived as threats to downstream neighbours and this tension often manifests in polarizing or nationalistic views between countries. Journalists attempting to balance these views must check their own biases and it is nearly impossible to cover all of our own blind spots at a very basic human level.

Developing a network of journalists who share an interest in promoting balanced news has been an important feature of SIWI's media workshops. Bringing together journalists from across borders to share experiences and views, the workshops become a platform for media colleagues to hear and reflect on the ways people from other countries may internalize certain topics.

In a river basin where water is shared by 11 distinctly different countries, journalists in the Nile can rely on each other as sounding boards for their own work. SIWI encourages constant dialogue and sharing between physical workshops through virtual platforms like Facebook or WhatsApp. These closed virtual meeting rooms have become a place for journalists to share stories among themselves, identify examples of troubling journalism, and to develop a shared understanding or vision of how journalism can support the cooperation process. After the most recent journalist workshop facilitated by SIWI in December 2019, the journalists engaged collectively developed a joint statement codifying their mutual interests.

Science Communication Skills for Water Coverage
Case study: IHE-SciDev Training

By Charles Wendo
SciDev.Net

Fig. 10.1. The Source of the Nile Bridge, also known as New Jinja Bridge, is a cable-stayed structure across the Victoria Nile in Jinja, Uganda. Photo by Fredrick Mugira.

For several decades, different media portals have been covering water from a national security perspective. This kind of narrative demonstrates how various media outlets report on water issues, which is that something needs to change, one way or another.

Naturally, it is easier to speak than to act; however, here, it is essential to act.

One way is to promote media coverage of research findings on numerous studies in various fields, such as hydrology, ecology and sociology along the Nile Basin.

Both scientists and journalists have a key role in this. Scientists need to make their research findings available for journalists to report on, so as to inform and influence policy makers. Research that is not communicated beyond the scientific audience might never reach policy makers and therefore might not influence policy.

Training

Training is one way of building the capacity and knowledge of journalists, to ensure better reporting. It comes in several forms and methodologies, and it is a continuously evolving process of learning by doing. Accurate and constructive media reporting of research findings essentially requires the attention and efforts of both scientists and journalists.

Through this chapter, I will shed light on an online course that took place between October 2018 and March 2019 in partnership between SciDev.Net and IHE Delft Institute for Water Education.

In May 2017, a workshop was held in Cairo, Egypt to explore ways in which researchers doing research on topics related to the Nile Basin can work with journalists, aiming for better communication of science through media. The workshop hosted 40 participants, including communication specialists, scientists, academics, policy makers and NGOs' representatives from Egypt, Ethiopia, Sudan and international organizations.

The workshop concluded that researchers and journalists needed more training in communicating and reporting science. Furthermore, participants pointed out the following:

- Scientific language is difficult for journalists, therefore it is essential to train scientists on how to simplify their jargon.
- Science communication training opportunities in the region come only occasionally, workshops need to be a more sustainable endeavour.
- Journalists and researchers in the region lack opportunities to network with one another and share ideas and experiences. Networking can be facilitated by bringing journalists, researchers and policy makers together during training and relevant conferences and events.
- There are trust issues between journalists and scientists, therefore training should help both sides to better understand each other.
- Language barriers make it harder to deliver training in the region. One of the ways to overcome this is to train local trainers, who will in turn train others in their respective countries.

- Online training platforms provide an excellent alternative to delivering training to scientists and journalists over broader geographical areas.
- Training handouts should be prepared to facilitate learning beyond the training days.

Fig. 10.2. The famous Cairo Tower, one of the tallest structures in Egypt, is situated very close from the Nile. Photo by Fredrick Mugira.

In this respect, IHE Delft Institute partnered with SciDev.Net to develop and run an online course, 'Science Communication Skills for Water Cooperation and Diplomacy'. The main objective was to build the capacity of scientists to engage with the media and effectively communicate science, and to deal with the River Nile as a vehicle of cooperation and development rather than conflict.

Course Development and Implementation

The course targeted researchers carrying out studies in fields of natural, applied and social sciences along the Nile Basin, whether or not they were based in the region. Based on the training needs identified at the Cairo workshop in 2017, along with in-depth interviews with stakeholders via conference calls in early 2018, the following modules were created:

Module 1: The media landscape and water diplomacy
Module 2: How to work with the media
Module 3: Making water science interesting to journalists and their audiences

Module 4: Simplifying your science
Module 5: Dealing with numbers and statistics
Module 6: Preparing media statements and press releases
Module 7: How to talk in public and to the press
Module 8: Developing a communications strategy

The modules were designed to take an average of 2–3 hours of the learner's online and offline time.

Although the course was intended for scientists carrying out research within the Nile Basin – and this was made clear in the announcement – it attracted participants from countries outside the region, such as Iran, the Palestinian Territories and Zambia. A total of 45 people from 18 countries were accepted to be enrolled in the course. Of these, 36 registered for the course, 27 introduced themselves, 16 commenced the course and 10 completed it.

The completion rate, taking the denominator as the number that actually commenced the course, rather than those who merely subscribed by logging in, was 10 out of 16, which is 63%. Free online courses tend to have low completion rates, often falling anywhere between 2% and 25%. One of the reasons people drop out of courses could be because they get too busy with other competing commitments. Indeed some participants gave feedback that the course was too long. Perhaps this is because some scientists look at media training and media relations as something to do in their spare time. Since the course is free, there is no money to lose by not completing the course when they get busier with their mainstream scientific work.

Strategies to retain participants included: keeping each module short, sending weekly reminders, promising a certificate, learning activities and discussion forums.

Of the 27 participants who introduced themselves, the majority were water, civil or environmental engineers (12). Six were specialists in water governance, management and hydropolitics. Five were in the media, communications and international relations. Three were environmental or ecological scientists, while one was a medical doctor specializing in water and sanitation issues.

Regarding their work placement, 17 were in academic institutions as lecturers, PhD students, Masters students or post-doctoral fellows. Ten were professionals in governmental or non-governmental sectors.

The course commenced on 22 October 2018. It was initially meant to close on 1 February 2019, but was extended to 1 March 2019 to enable a few more participants finish.

Key Learning from the Course

Most participants indicated that the course met their expectations, taught them how media works and helped them communicate science to non-specialists. The table below summarises their responses.

Statement	Agree	Neutral	Disagree
This course has helped me to understand how media works in my country (or in the country where I work) and how to communicate my work more effeciently	7	1	1
I now have a better understanding of how my work fits into the communication of water science relating to the Nile Basin and the 'wider debate on water conflicts and cooperation'	8	1	0
The course has taught me how to communicate statistics, in a way that makes them interesting, relevant, and accessible	4	2	3
I learnt how to get key messages across to journalists and ensure that my work gets reported on accurately	8	1	0
The course has taught me how to speak publicly and ways to come across as confident and engaging	7	1	1
After this course, I am now more confident to communicate my work over social media	8	0	1

Conclusion

Overall, the course had largely met the desired objectives. Most respondents greatly appreciated practical exercises, especially those on writing a press release and designing a communication strategy. The training platform was accessible and easy to use for most participants.

However, there were areas that didn't work as expected, most notably the length of the course. Clearly many scientists wanted to learn science communication but didn't want to spend 16–24 hours on it.

It might be necessary in the future to increase the number of accepted candidates in the beginning, to compensate for the dropout of some of them later. Also, it has been clear from the feedback that participants prefer more engagement with the trainers, for instance through Skype calls and online discussions.

Break-away text: How to simplify scientific information for journalists

Scientists should be aware that most journalists do not have a scientific background. The same concept should apply in communicating science to non-specialized audiences, which is why journalists should offer their stories in a very simple, yet interesting way. The following are tips for scientists to best communicate their work:

- Avoid scientific jargon as much as possible. Use alternative common words and phrases whenever possible.
- If you have to use technical words or expressions, explain them.
- Compare sizes, shapes, colours, etc. with something your audience can visualize.

- Use numbers and statistics sparingly, and in rather a simple format, unless the precise figure is necessary.
- Use images – photos, infographics and infovideos.
- Avoid information overload: just focus on your main research findings and their implications.

Break-away text: Ways to make science interesting to journalists and the public
Journalists are more likely to report on research findings if they find them interesting, important and timely enough to draw the attention of their listeners, viewers and readers. The following are useful tips for scientists to communicate their findings to journalists:

- Link your research findings to a trending topic where possible. Use science to provide an explanation, expert opinion or advice on the trending topic.
- Humanize the story: Show the impact of a scientific development or phenomena by telling the real life story of an affected person or group of people.
- Show how your research findings are relevant to everyday life, such as how this research reflects on things like food, utilities, income, health, education, family relations and happiness.
- Provide them with amazing facts or figures to capture their attention.
- Get a famous person to speak about your topic.
- Tell the story of something amazing or fascinating that happened during the course of your work.

Fig. 10.3. People aboard a boat in Blue Nile, Khartoum Sudan. The River Nile plays a vital role in transportation of people and goods in the Nile Basin. Photo by Fredrick Mugira.

Printed and bound by CPI Group (UK) Ltd, Croydon, CR0 4YY
22/03/2026

14847627-0001